Handbook of Foams

Also by Francisco Aragón (translator)

POETRY

After Rubén
His Tongue a Swath of Sky (chapbook)
Glow of Our Sweat
Puerta del Sol
Tertulia (chapbook)
In Praise of Cities (chapbook)
Light, Yogurt, Strawberry Milk (chapbook)

TRANSLATIONS

From the Other Side of Night
Sonnets to Madness and Other Misfortunes
Of Dark Love
Body in Flames
Lorca: Selected Verse (co-translator)
Federico García Lorca: *Collected Poems* (co-translator)

Gerardo Diego

Handbook of Foams
Manual de espumas

translated from Spanish by
Francisco Aragón

Shearsman Books

First published in the United Kingdom in 2026 by
Shearsman Books Ltd
PO Box 4239
Swindon
SN3 9FN

Shearsman Books Ltd Registered Office
30–31 St. James Place, Mangotsfield, Bristol BS16 9JB
(this address not for correspondence)

EU AUTHORISED REPRESENTATIVE:
Lightning Source France, 1 Av. Johannes Gutenberg, 78310 Maurepas, France
Email: compliance@lightningsource.fr

www.shearsman.com

ISBN 978-1-84861-986-9

Original text copyright © Herederos de Gerardo Diego
Translation copyright © Francisco Aragón, 2026

The right of Francisco Aragón to be identified as the translator of this work has been asserted by him in accordance with the Copyrights, Designs and Patents Act of 1988. All rights reserved.

Acknowledgements
The editions used for the Spanish originals of these poems are:

Gerardo Diego: *Poesía completa*, Vol. 1.
Edición de F. J. de Revenga. Valencia, Editorial Pre-Textos, 2017

Gerardo Diego: *Manual de espumas*
Madrid, Cuadernos Literarios, 1924
(facsimile edition produced by Editorial Pre-Textos, Valencia, 2007)

Contents

	Francisco Aragón: Contextualizing *Handbook of Foams*	7
18	Primavera / Spring	19
20	Mirador / Lookout	21
22	Emigrante / Emigrant	23
24	Mesa / Table	25
26	Fuente / Fountain	27
28	Paraíso / Paradise	29
32	Canción fluvial / River Song	33
38	Rima / Rhyme	39
40	Otoño / Autumn	41
42	Noche de reyes / Twelfth Night	43
46	Bahía / Bay	47
50	Recital / Recital	51
52	Pueblo / Village	53
54	Hotel / Hotel	55
58	Canción de cuna / Lullaby	59
60	Vendimia / Grape Harvest	61
62	Adiós / Goodbye	63
64	Novela / Novel	65
68	Nieve / Snow	69
70	Panorama / Panorama	71
72	Nubes / Clouds	73
76	Cuadro / Painting	77
78	Camino / Road	79
82	Alegoría / Allegory	83
84	Nocturno / Nocturne	85
86	Pasión penúltima / Penultimate Passion	87
88	Eco / Echo	89
90	Lluvia / Rain	91
92	Ventana / Window	93
94	Espectáculo / Performance	95
	Francisco Aragón: *Mostly Madrid*	98
	Publication credits	110
	Gratitude	111
	Biographical sketches	113

Contextualizing *Handbook of Foams*

(July 1925)

Dear Poet

I received your nice letter shortly after you posted it. You have nothing to thank me for. We have you to thank since we were able to award a beautiful book. It's a shame you didn't enter Handbook of Foams... *Marvelous your* Handbook of Foams. *In my judgement, the highest achievement of the new lyric.*
  See you soon.
    Yours
    Antonio Machado [1]

Gerardo Diego (1896–1987) was born in the north of Spain in Santander, the capital of Cantabria—a region which, along with Galicia, the Basque Country and Asturias make up what's often called *la España verde* for its lush landscapes. Although Diego spent most of his professional life in Madrid, his works often engage the seascapes of the north, including his critically acclaimed volume, *Handbook of Foams*—a thirty-poem suite, or "concerto" as one scholar has called it.[2]

Diego, in addition to being a poet, was an accomplished pianist and music critic. Music and the sea are motifs that insinuate themselves throughout *Handbook*—all under the banner of what literary critics came to call *creacionismo*, whose most well-known adherent was the Chilean poet Vicente Huidobro (1893–1948). Octavio Paz (1914–1998) once said of him: "He is everywhere and nowhere. He is the invisible oxygen of our poetry." [3]

1916 is a dual threshold of sorts for poetry in the Spanish language. On the one hand, Rubén Darío (1867–1916), the master of *modernismo*, abandons Europe to return to his native Nicaragua and dies, marking the decline of this symbolist aesthetic. On the other, a young Vicente Huidobro departs from Santiago, Chile for Paris, France to absorb the artistic innovations percolating there, intent on becoming one of its most flamboyant ambassadors.

But first he stops in Madrid, where he meets Rafael Cansinos-Asséns (1882–1964), who introduces him to Ramón Gómez de la Serna (1888–1963): they are, these two, the overseers of what's new in Spanish letters—

friendly rivals who hold court at their respective *tertulias* at Café Colonial and Café Pombo. But Huidobro decides to keep to himself certain notions. Had he felt more secure, he might have shared the gist of a talk he gave in Chile two years prior, in which he stated:

> We've accepted, without giving it much thought, that there can't be other realities except those that surround us, and we haven't stopped to think that we too can create realities in a world of our own, a world that is waiting for its own flora and fauna.[4]

Huidobro's tentative ideas around what he terms *creacionismo* are solidified by the time he reappears in Madrid in 1918 after his two-year stint in Paris—a stint during which he meets and mingles with the likes of Apollinaire, Pierre Reverdy, Pablo Picasso, and Juan Gris.[5]

He sets up a literary salon at his home on Plaza Oriente opposite the Royal Palace. The frequent gatherings take place from August to November. Huidobro's residence in Madrid becomes *the* place to be if you want to learn and sample what's new in the arts. In his book on Apollinaire, Spanish avant-garde poet and critic Guillermo de Torre recalls:

> Where did I hear of him, or read him for the first time?… I don't think I would be mistaken if I said it was at Vicente Huidobro's house.[6]

During these months in Madrid, Huidobro manages the feat of publishing four collections of poetry, including *Arctic Poems*, which Antonio Machado reviews in a piece titled "Images in the lyric (on the margins of Vicente Huidobro's book)." Gerardo Diego doesn't meet the Chilean poet during this period but he does read Machado's review with great interest.[7] Of Huidobro's stay, the aforementioned Cansinos-Asséns wrote:

> …his arrival in Madrid was the only literary happening of the year, because with him the latest literary tendencies from abroad came our way; and he assumed the representation of one of them, not the least interesting, creacionismo….[8]

1919 marks Gerardo Diego's decisive trip Madrid, not to meet Vicente Huidobro yet but rather to immerse himself in Huidobro's wake: *ultraísmo*, Spain's branch of the European avant-garde. Diego will recall in 1948:

A few months later, and as a result of his visit, *ultraísmo* was born, and the fuss that was being made in Spain was unleashed. Controversies, lectures, magazines, books, articles, manifestos...[2]

Ultraísmo, more than offering a specific literary model, creates the ambiance Gerardo Diego intuitively needs, at least for a time, to point him in new directions. Through friends, he gets to meet (like Huidobro before him) Rafael Cansinos-Asséns, which of course leads to further contacts. At Cansinos-Asséns' *tertulia*, for example, he encounters a young Argentinean named Jorge Luis Borges, with whom he will share the Cervantes Prize, Spanish letters' highest honor, in 1979. And he also meets a poet from Granada named Federico García Lorca. One self-proclaimed *ultraísta*, Eugenio Montes[10] —who will eventually review *Handbook of Foams* in the prestigious journal *Revista de Occidente*—loans Diego a copy of *Arctic Poems*, from which he copies out three he especially likes, including one titled 'Moon.' When Gerardo Diego heads back to Santander he takes a short detour to Bilbao to see the poet, Juan Larrea. In addition to the three hand-copied poems, Diego is carrying the magazines *Grecia* and *Cervantes*, harboring the hunch that these will impress his Basque friend. At a symposium on Huidobro that will take place in Chicago in 1978, Larrea will recall what 'Moon' meant to him, saying, "its reading plunged me into an atmosphere of ultraworld..." He will sum up the materials Diego brought to Bilbao by saying, "The novelty impressed me in such a way that from that day on I began to feel like another person."[11]

Dámaso Alonso, the most scholarly poet of Diego's generation (commonly known as the "generation of '27"), and who went on to preside over the Royal Spanish Academy many years later, would write that although *ultraísmo*, as a movement, did not produce great poets, modern Spanish poetry could not be fully understood without taking *ultraísmo* into account. The only *books* that survived, in Alonso's view, were two: *Image* and *Handbook of Foams*, both by Gerardo Diego. These collections were the result, though only in part, of Diego's contact with *ultraísmo* and its challenge to "go beyond." Diego says:

> I invented my own *ultraísmo* in Santander. I began to write poems in a somewhat systematic way in 1918 and I alternated very naïve poems... with others that were more adventurous, which I'd write for pleasure and without restrictions, not trying to penetrate the secret of the classics, but rather, on the contrary, trying to discover poetry's new worlds. (Bernal 14)

More than the literary politics and posturing playing out in Madrid, Diego's primary field of exploration is Vicente Huidobro's poetry and his correspondence with Juan Larrea.

Towards the end of 1919 Gerardo Diego delivers two lectures in Santander. "The New Poetry" is about the *isms* flaring around Europe, and "Poetic and Artistic Renovation" presents Spain's *ultraísmo*. Both make more than a few waves, spurring debate in favor and against the new trends taking shape. But Diego doesn't consider himself a militant in the classical sense. One specialist sees his association with the *ultraistas* as only one part of his "poetic biography:"

> In truth, Diego, despite his *ultraist* posture, or in addition to it, irreversibly consolidates throughout 1921 a process that was initiated in 1919 and which, in theory and practice, was kept afloat by Larrea; which consisted in a personal apprehension and assimilation of Huidobro's *creacionismo*, whose books he devoured and commented with his close Basque friend (Bernal 41)

Diego finally decides to write to Huidobro in 1920, sending him a copy of one of his essays and an extensive poem dedicated to him titled 'Gesta,' which will form part of *Image*, his first avant-garde book. But here's the thing: even before Gerardo Diego mails these materials to Vicente Huidobro, the Chilean has already heard of him. It's a time when everyone is writing to Huidobro and in the letters he receives from Madrid a *"creacionista" (not ultraísta)* named Gerardo Diego is sometimes mentioned. Huidobro's curiosity is piqued and he asks a Spanish friend to send him a few of Diego's poems.[12]

In April of the following year, 1921, Madrid's newsstands are displaying the first issue of *Creación*, an art magazine edited by Huidobro from Paris. In it there is a poem by Diego titled 'Cold,' a poem Huidobro will cite in his extensive prose piece, 'Creacionismo,' which will be published in his book, *Manifestes*, in 1925.

To set the record straight, then: *creacionismo* was *not* a one-man school, as two of Vicente Huidobro's translators into English, both American, have written. In fact, in a 1923 interview for the Paris journal *L'esprit nouveau*, Huidobro himself mentions "the creationist poets Juan Larrea and Gerardo Diego, two great poets." One Hispanist has referred to Huidobro, Diego and Larrea as "the creationist triad."[13]

In the Autumn of 1921, Huidobro writes to Diego, expressing his wish to give a talk in Madrid on *creacionismo*. Diego confers with a friend on the board of the Atheneum and a date is set for December. Both Diego and Larrea are finally going to meet who they consider their mentor. Larrea is living in Madrid working at the National Historic Archive while Diego, teaching high school French in Soria, will travel to the capital by train. They attend Huidobro's lecture and notice that the *ultraístas* give the Chilean a cool reception. This is due, in part, to the dispute over who was the "founder" of *creacionismo*: Pierre Reverdy or Vicente Huidobro? Reverdy's camp is spearheaded by the *ultraístas'* most militant activist, Guillermo de Torre,[14] who will publish his important study, *European Avant-Garde Literatures* in 1925, the year that *Handbook of Foams* finds its way into print.

Diego remains in Madrid for only a day, so it is Larrea who gets to talk at length with Huidobro. The author of *Handbook of Foams* will have his chance when he's invited to Paris. In late Summer/early Autumn of the following year Gerardo Diego spends sixteen days in the French capital. There are two letters addressed to Larrea—one dated September 5, 1922 from Paris and the other October 7, 1922 from Gijón—that scholars have scrutinized to better understand the context from which *Handbook of Foams* emerged.[15]

Although relatively brief, the letter from Paris touches upon key elements of *Handbook*'s origins: Vicente Huidobro's work, Juan Gris' cubism, and music. Other information is incidental: Diego departed for Paris from San Sebastian on August 31; Huidobro was waiting for him at the train station; the weather was bad, dissuading them from any sightseeing. A more interesting observation is that Huidobro seems to know everybody. They have a couple of meals with Juan Gris and visit his studio, and he mentions that they are set to have lunch with Erik Satie and Maurice Raynal, an art critic associated with the cubists.

The letter from Gijón is considerably more substantial. In reference to the attitude in Paris, at least Huidobro's, towards musicians, Diego writes:

> They look down on musicians as primitives—we've discussed this quite a bit, Huidobro can't conceive that I like music—only Erik Satie, Auric, and a few others are partially saved…

On Juan Gris he writes:

> We found him working in his studio. He showed me his things and from that day on we had lunch together often and we had long talks. He's an admirable [...] conscientious artist who judges

universal art and his own work with a clarity that is mathematical... Listening to him speak of aesthetics, I have learned to catch a glimpse of what painting is, and in this sense I do understand his work, that is: it produces in me an impression of sober and delicate beauty, of mature and reposed construction...

Gerardo Diego will go on to dedicate the longest poem in *Handbook of Foams*, 'River Song,' to Juan Gris. 1996 marks the centenary of Diego's birth and the long-standing journal, *Revista de Occidente*, publishes a special number titled 'Gerardo Diego and the invention of new poetry', which includes an article titled 'Gerardo Diego's cubist fascination.'[16] The article discusses the correlation between Gris' paintings and Diego's verse, above all in *Handbook*. On Huidobro's poetics Diego writes:

> This plastic technique in Huidobro's poetry has shed much light on his work, though I wouldn't know how to specify with precision the *"why"* but could only tell you about it in general terms. The principal of the *rapport* is the hub of it... It's the same thing we saw in him in Madrid, but it's clearer to me now after seeing cubism. Nothing can go without its *"why"* and the artist should know at all times the values of the measures and elements he employs...[17]

Diego has said it on more than one occasion: Huidobro's creationist work has cubist painting as its model, while his own avant-garde verse, in addition to cubism, adds music as a guiding star. This particular excerpt lends weight to the notion that Diego's innovative work is not surrealist: it clearly rejects the idea of "automatic writing." Diego continues:

> I saw at the Opera *Boris Godunof*, Mussorgsky's famous opera. Music that is purely musical has never moved me with such intensity, like certain passages that were virtually paradisical. I almost wept with joy, not with melancholy or enthusiasm, which is how I usually get drunk with music.

In one of his notes,[18] Diego specialist José Luis Bernal writes: "This letter offers, as well, a very interesting piece of data about Diego's musical preferences in contrast with pictorial cubism's rigid tastes, which is key for a correct reading of *Handbook of Foams*, the true fruit of that experience."

Diego will point out many years later the importance of his musical background in this book's elaboration.[19] Before citing a final fragment from this letter, I would like to call attention to something written by the late José Hierro, arguably the Spanish poet most influenced by Gerardo Diego:

> *Creacionismo* would be a way out for a classical disposition, bashful with its feelings, incapable therefore, of expressing itself with the blind, romantic, immodesty of surrealism. But Gerardo Diego's great contribution, what distinguishes him from the others, is that despite appearances, his *creacionismo* is not an experience that is more or less amusing and ingenious, but rather a form — irrationalist—of confession.[20]

Gerardo Diego, in commenting on his *Handbook*, says: "It's possible that these poems, to the reader, seem cold, but I remember very well the blood they cost me."[21] With all this in mind, the final excerpt from Diego's letter of October 7, 1922 seems to suggests the poet's mood, or point of departure, in at least a handful of the poems in this collection:

> This summer's great sentimental failure marked me more than I thought; thankfully this trip has been a purification. But now, in the obligatory solitude of this indifferent, hard-working, cheery, superficial city, pessimistic and misanthropic thoughts, when not of a lower nature, assault me. I'm convinced I'm an ill-bred child and that without any luck, my life will be empty and miserable. It's been 20 days with no sign of friendship or love. If this doesn't change soon, I think I'll emigrate. Meanwhile, and filled with resignation, I read novels and go to the movies: two absurdities.

Diego has just turned 26. With the exception of 'Spring'—which opens *Manual de espumas*—he is about to write, under a melancholic spell perhaps, the twenty-nine poems that will complete the collection that concerns us. That summer Diego is living in a beach bungalow in the coastal city of Gijón in Asturias, from which he is able to glimpse the Cantabrian sea.

Towards the end of the letter he says: "I haven't written anything new." Juan Larrea, his dear friend and fellow *creacionista*, would have been the first to know if he had.

Nearly two months later, in a letter to another close friend, José María de Cossío, author of the classic encyclopedia on bullfighting, Gerardo Diego reveals: "I've just put the finishing touches on a new creature that aspires to be a book of poems, born *Handbook of Foams*."[22]

*

Notes

[1] This letter was reproduced in a special homage issue of *Punta Europa* #112–113, Madrid, in 'Tres Cartas a Gerardo Diego'. Antonio Machado is referring to the National Poetry Prize, which Gerardo Diego won that year with a manuscript of traditional verse titled *Poemas Humanos*. He did not enter *Handbook of Foams* because it did not have the minimum number of required pages.
[2] The scholar in question is José Luis Bernal, whose edited volume, *Gerardo Diego y la Vanguardia Hispánica* (Universidad de Extrema-dura, 1993) was a key source for this piece.
[3] Cited in 'Poetry is a Heavenly Crime,' David M. Guss' Introduction to *The Selected Poetry of Vicente Huidobro* (New Directions, New York, 1981).
[4] Huidobro's 'Manifiesto non serviam,' cited in 'Teoría del Creacionismo' by Antonio de Undurraga, which prologues *Poesía y Prosa* (Aguilar, 1957).
[5] For Huidobro's exploits in Paris, David M. Guss is a place to start. From there, René de Costa's book, *Huidobro: The Careers of a Poet* (Oxford University Press, 1984), is a thorough study and account.
[6] He also affirms that it was at Huidobro's house that *ultraísmo*, Spain's avant-garde movement of the period, was "incubated." *Apollinaire y las teorías del cubismo* (EDHASA, Barcelona, 1967).
[7] René de Costa's paper, 'Posibilidades Creacionistas,' is a primary source for much of this. It can be found in the aforementioned *Gerardo Diego y la Vanguardia Hispánica*, 1993.
[8] 'Un Gran Poeta Chileno: Vicente Huidobro y el Creacionismo' (1919) by Rafael Cansinos-Asséns, included in *Vicente Huidobro y el Creacionismo* edited by René de Costa (Taurus Ediciones, Madrid, 1975).
[9] The first exhibition devoted entirely to *ultraísmo* was held in Valencia, Spain, between June and September of 1996 under the organization of Juan Manuel Bonet, a specialist in the movement who prepared the text and notes for the handsome catalogue, which included a complete English translation. *El Ultraísmo y las artes plásticas*, Centro Julio González 27 Junio – 8 Septiembre.
[10] Montes would later abandon the *ultraist* aesthetic, and adopt fascist politics.
[11] *La Biografía Ultraísta de Gerardo Diego* by José Luis Bernal (Universidad de Extremadura, Cáceres, 1987). This 60-page study is another primary source for much of this. This citation is taken from the article 'Vicente Huidobro en

Vanguardia' in *Revista Ibero-americana*, v. XLV #106–107, 1979. Further citations from this study are indicated in the text in parenthesis, i.e. (Bernal 41).

[12] See note 7 above.

[13] Robert Guerney, in 'El Creacionismo de Juan Larrea,' is the Hispanist in question, in *Gerardo Diego y la Vanguardia Hispánica*, 1993. David Bary, in his book *Nuevos Estudios sobre Huidobro y Larrea* (Pre-textos, Valencia, 1984) cites the interview in issue #18 of *L'Esprit Nouveau*, in which Huidobro names Larrea and Diego as *creacionistas*.

[14] Many years later, Guillermo de Torre writes that his position on Huidobro had to do with his youthful activism and his way of countering Huidobro's ego, which even his friends admitted was considerable. In fact, in 1962, he writes an article—'La Polémica del Creacionismo: Huidobro y Reverdy,' included in *Vicente Huidobro y el Creacionismo* (Taurus) — in which he persuasively argues that neither Huidobro nor Reverdy had a monopoly on their avant-garde poetic; painters and writers of the period were saying more or less the same thing: that the artist had to create a new reality and not describe or imitate the reality before them....

[15] "Desteñidas Esquelas. Charlas Líricas. Algunas cartas de Gerardo Diego a Juan Larrea" commented by José Luis Bernal and Juan Manuel Díaz de Guereñu, *Insula* #586, 1995.

[16] *Revista de Occidente* #178 Marzo, 1996, a special issue titled "Gerardo Diego y la invención de la poesía nueva." The article's author is Teresa Hernández.

[17] Just before citing a brief fragment of Huidobro's lecture in Madrid in 1921, René de Costa writes: "In this way, Huidobro constructs a text which forces the reader to associate ideas and establish the lexical contacts which make the metaphors detonate, creating a new and sparkling language in the process, a new way of poeticizing." The fragment: "The poet makes things in nature change their lifestyle, retrieving with his net everything that moves in the chaos of the unnameable, hanging electric wires between words, remote spaces suddenly lighting up... " *Vicente Huidobro: Poesía y poética* (1911–1948), Antología comentada por René de Costa (Alianza, Madrid, 1996).

[18] See note 15.

[19] In '*De la musique avant toute chose*: la evolución del pentagrama en la poesía de Gerardo Diego,' Gabriele Morelli writes: "The process in which the phonic effects require a substantial structural value in the message, to the point of representing the very reality of the poetic discourse, is carried out completely in the creationist experience of *Handbook of Foams*."

[20] 'Entrañable Gerardo' by José Hierro in a special homage issue of *Punta Europa* # 112–13, Madrid, 1966.

[21] Ricardo Gullón cites this statement of Diego's in 'La Veta Aventurera de Gerardo Diego' in *Insula* #90, 1953.

[22] Gerardo Diego / José María de Cossío. *Epistolario. Nuevas Claves de la Generación del 27* Edición de Rafael Gómez de (Ediciones de la Universidad de Alcalá de Henares, 1996).

Sobre la tumba inesperada de
JOSÉ DE CIRIA ESCALANTE,
amigo indeleble, estos versos
que él amaba, hoy con voluntad de flores

PLACED UPON THE UNEXPECTED TOMB OF
JOSÉ DE CIRIA ESCALANTE.
INDELIBLE FRIEND, THESE POEMS
WHICH HE LOVED, ASPIRE TO BE FLOWERS

Primavera

A Melchor Fernández Almagro

Ayer   Mañana
Los días niños cantan en mi ventana

Las casas son todas de papel
y van y vienen las golondrinas
doblando y desdoblando esquinas

Violadores de rosas
Gozadores perpetuos del marfil de las cosas
Ya tenéis aquí el nido
que en la más bella grúa se os ha construido

Y desde él cantaréis todos
en las manos del viento

                  Mi vida es un limón
            pero no es amarilla mi canción
                Limones y planetas
                en las ramas del sol
            Cuántas veces cobijasteis
              la sombra verde de mi amor
              la sombra verde de mi amor

La primavera nace
y en su cuerpo de luz la lluvia pace

El arco iris brota de la cárcel

Y sobre los tejados
mi mano blanca es un hotel
para palomas de mi cielo infiel

Spring

for Melchor Fernández Almagro

Yesterday   Tomorrow
The child-like days sing at my window

The houses are made of paper
and the swallows come and go
turning and re-turning corners

Ravishers of roses
Forever enjoying things ivory
Here you have now the nest
built for you on the most beautiful crane

And from it you will all sing
in the hands of the wind

                    My life is a lemon
               though my song isn't yellow
                  Lemons and planets
                  on the sun's branches
              Oh the times you've sheltered
                my love's green shade
                my love's green shade

Spring arrives
and rain grazes on her body of light

A rainbow arcs from the jail

And on the roofs
my pale hand's a hotel
for the pigeons of my unfaithful sky

Mirador

A Ramón Gómez de la Serna

De balcón a balcón
los violines de ciego
tienden sus arcos de pasión

Es algo irremediable
cortar con las tijeras estas calles

Las cartas nacidas de mi regazo
aprenden a volar algo mejor
y a un peregrino arrepentido
se le ha visto bajar en ascensor

En el bazar
las banderas renuevan el aire
y el caballo de copas lleva el paso
mejor que un militar

Y tú   manso tranvía
gusano de mis lágrimas
que hilas mi llanto en tus entrañas

Condúceme a tu establo
y sácame del pozo en que te hablo

Yo te prometo que esta primavera
tu vara florezca en todos los tejados
tejados olvidados
en los que ya no pastan los ganados
y a los que nunca sube el surtidor

Dejemos al Señor
que arranque las estrellas
y durmámonos
sin consultar con ellas

Lookout

for Ramón Gómez de la Serna

From balcony to balcony
the violins of the blind lay
their bows of passion down

Shearing these streets with scissors
is something you can't avoid

The letters written in my lap
learn to fly a little better
and someone's seen a sorry pilgrim
in a descending lift

At the bazaar
flapping flags renew the air
and the Jack of Hearts marches
better than a soldier

And you   gentle streetcar
worm of my tears
that spins my grief in your very core

Drive me to your stable and pull me
from the well from which I speak

I promise your trolley will bloom
on every roof this spring
forgotten roofs
where cattle no longer graze
where the jet's spray doesn't reach

Leave it to the Lord
to pluck constellations
and let's fall asleep
without consulting the stars

Emigrante

El viento vuelve siempre
aunque cada vez traiga un color diferente

Y los niños del lugar
danzan alrededor de las nuevas cometas

                                  Canta cometa canta
                                  con las alas abiertas
                                      y lánzate a volar
                            pero nunca te olvides de tus trenzas

Las cometas pasaron
pero sus sombras quedan colgadas de las puertas
y el rastro que dejaron
fertiliza las huertas

Por los surcos del mar
ni una sola semilla deja de brotar
Chafadas por los vientos y los barcos
las espumas reflorecen todos los años

Pero yo amo más bien
los montes que conducen sobre sus lomos ágiles
las estrellas expulsadas del harem

Pastor marino
que sin riendas ni bridas
guías las olas a su destino
No me dejes sentado en el camino

El viento vuelve siempre
Las cometas también
Gotas de sangre de sus trenzas llueven
Y yo monto en el tren

Emigrant

The wind always returns
though each time brings a different color

And local children dance
around new kites

                                      Sing kite sing
                         with your wings spread wide
                          and hurl yourself in flight
                  though never forget your braids

The kites came and went
yet their shadows still hang on doors
and the trails they left behind
still fertilize the fields

In the furrows of the sea
not a single seed fails to sprout
Flattened by the winds and boats
the foams reflower each year

But I prefer the hills
that carry on their agile backs
the stars expelled from their harem

Shepherd of the sea
who without rein or bridle
guides the waves to their fate
Don't leave me sitting beside the road

The wind always returns
The kites too
Drops of blood fall from their braids
And I board the train

Mesa

A Waldemar George

Yo recorrí los mares
embarcado en tu mano
y en los manteles puse un sabor de océano

Los peces giran en torno de mi faro
Pero los barcos naufragaban en el mapa
y el rumor de las olas desplegaba mi capa

El mar ya no se cuida de ser redondo

No penséis en la muerte

No es fácil llegar al fondo
ni hacer de nuestra alfombra la rueda de la suerte

El sol nace en la mesa
y el árbol del poniente pierde las hojas viejas

                Ésta es la cruz del mar
                Nunca crece ni mengua

Esperad que la lámpara se oriente

Y entonces nuestros platos
girarán bellamente
a la música exacta de los astros

Table

for Waldemar George

I travelled the seas
on the boat of your hand
leaving on tablecloths an ocean taste

Fish wheel around my lighthouse
But boats were wrecking on maps
and the murmur of the waves spreading my cape

The sea no longer bothers being round

Snatch your mind off death

It isn't easy getting to the bottom
nor rendering our rug a wheel of fortune

The sun rises off the table
and the sunset's tree sheds its withered leaves

        This is the sea's cross
        It never waxes or wanes

Wait for the lamp to steady itself

And only then will our plates
turn beautifully
to the precise music of the stars

Fuente

Mecanismo de amor
Mi grifo versifica mejor que el ruiseñor

Y eras tú y tu vestido
lo que todos los días he bebido

                                       camino de la noche
                                         junto al árbol real
                                 mientras el viento espera
                             la hora de abrir el hospital

Pero tus ojos ya no vuelan
y las últimas ventanas están muertas

El agua en el balcón
como un perro olvidado

Mi corazón y el baño se vacían

Puedes dormir tranquila
                     No hay cuidado

Fountain

Contraption of love
My faucet versifies better than a nightingale

And it was you and your dress
I drank from every day

                                  road of the night
                               beside the royal tree
                                while the wind awaits
                         the hospital's opening hour

But your eyes no longer soar
and the last windows are dead

The water on the balcony
like a forgotten dog

My heart and the tub empty out

You can sleep in peace
                        No need to worry

Paraíso

A J. Moreno Villa

Danzar
                Cautivos del bar

La vida es una torre
y el sol un palomar
Lancemos las camisas tendidas a volar

Por el piano arriba
subamos con los pies frescos de cada día

Hay que dejar atrás
las estelas oxidadas
y el humo casi florecido

Hay que llegar sin hacer ruido

Bien saben los remeros
con sus alas de insecto que no pueden cantar
Y que su proa no se atrevió a volar

Ellos son los pacientes hilanderos de rías
fumadores tenaces de espumas y de días

Danzar
                Cautivos del bar

Porque las nubes cantan
aunque estén siempre abatidas las alas de la mar

De un lado a otro del mundo
los arcoiris van y vienen
para vosotros todos
los que perdisteis los trenes

Paradise

for J. Moreno Villa

Let's dance
                Captives in the bar

Life is a tower
and the sun a pigeon house
Let's fling the drying shirts into flight

Let's climb the piano upstairs
with fresh everyday feet

We have to leave behind
the rusted wake
and the smoke that almost flowered

We must arrive without a sound

With their insect wings the rowers
know very well they can't sing
and their prows didn't risk flight

They patiently spin river mouths
tenaciously smoke days and foams

Let's dance
                Captives in the bar

Because the clouds can sing
though waves of the sea lay low in defeat

From one side of the world to the other
rainbows come and go
for those of you
who missed your train

Y también por vosotros
mi flauta hace girar los árboles
y el crepúsculo alza
los pechos y los mármoles

Las nubes son los pájaros
y el sol el palomar

Hurra
 Cautivos del bar

La vida es una torre
que crece cada día sobre el nivel del mar

For the rest of you as well
my flute twirls the trees
and marble and breasts
are hoisted at dawn

The clouds are birds
and the sun a pigeon house

Hurray
                        Captives in the bar

Life is a tower
rising daily over the sea

Canción fluvial

A Juan Gris

Por las praderas giratorias
pasa sólo una vez el río taciturno
cuando la noche toca su disco de gramófono
y los pájaros cuelgan de los árboles mustios

Aún las últimas gotas de luna
perfuman de alcoholes los mantos de la bruma
y el tren que iba bendiciendo el panorama
no perdió los kilómetros ni el compás de la ruta

Pero dejemos esto
y desciframos bien este libro de texto
que el sol nos ha legado
con una sola página herida en el costado

La araña telegráfica
distribuye la noche
y mientras en su jaula de cristal
reposa el pozo vecinal
yo veo que la estrella y el multicopiador
enojan al poeta que ha volado al portal

Hay que cambiar de rumbo
y como quien se lleva las flores del paisaje
cargar sobre los hombros el lírico equipaje

Surtidores maduros
que ofrecéis en las márgenes
vuestros intactos frutos
Es preciso pasar como los vientos castos
sin coger de los árboles los astros

River Song

for Juan Gris

Near the whirling prairies
as the night plays its record
and birds hang from withered trees
the river flows past once in silence

Final drops of moon still perfume
the shrouds of mist with liquor and the train
blessing the scene hasn't misplaced
the miles or the rhythm of the route

But forget about that and let's
properly decipher this text
the sun has handed down
one page of its flank a wound

The telegraphic spider
sends out the night
and as a local well relaxes
in its cage of glass
the multicopier and star enrage
the poet who's flown to the gate

We have to change course
and like those in the country picking flowers
carry lyrical luggage on our shoulders

Ripe fountains
offering on the side
your intact fruit
It's key you move like chaste winds
not plucking stars from trees

Mirad las lavanderas
nutriendo de colores las limpias faltriqueras

La espuma que levantan
sube a la misma altura
que esa copla que cantan

      La luna muele estrellas
      sin música y sin agua
      y el amor aburrido
        sube y baja

      La marea es tu vientre
      traspasado de gracia
      y el amor desde el nido
        rueda rueda
      como el molino turbio
        de la arboleda

Y por todo recuerdo
en el bolsillo mío el rumor de la presa
y un sabor de jabón en el remanso

      Los puentes fatigados
      sobre la orilla derecha
     duermen en espiral como los gatos

Tan sólo los devotos pescadores
se arrodillan y esperan
que de su caña broten flores y banderas

La noche se derrama
y rompe el horizonte

Estamos terminando el drama

Look at the laundresses
their clean petticoats feeding on colors

The foam they produce
rises as high
as that song they sing

                              The moon grinds stars
                              without music or water
                              and idle love
                                            rises and falls

                              The tide is your womb
                              transfixed with grace
                              and from its nest love
                                        spins and spins
                              like the muddy mill
                                  in the woods

And for each memory
in my pocket the murmur of the dam
and a taste of backwater soap

                              The tired bridges sleep
                                  on the riverbank
                                    curled like cats

Only the devoted fishermen
kneel and wait
for flowers and flags to sprout from their poles

Night spills
and splits the horizon

We're bringing this drama to a close

Los puentes de resorte
caminan de sur a norte

Y mi barca se ha dormido
sin hacer ruido

Una hora sube al cielo

Y en la cruz hacen su nido
la golondrina y mi pañuelo

Son las brisas del mar
las que cierran la noche y mi cantar

The bridges go forth
walking south to north

And my boat has fallen asleep
without making a sound

An hour floats up to the sky

The swallow and my handkerchief
nest on the cross

A breeze coming off the sea
is what ends the night and my song

Rima

Homenaje a Bécquer

Tus ojos oxigenan los rizos de la lluvia
y cuando el sol se pone en tus mejillas
tus cabellos no mojan ni la tarde es ya rubia

    Amor   Apaga la luna

No bebas tus palabras
ni viertas en mi vaso tus ojeras amargas
La mañana de verte se ha puesto morena

    Enciende el sol   Amor
y mata la verbena

Rhyme

Homage to Bécquer

Your eyes breathe in the rain's curls
and when the sun sets on your cheeks
your hair doesn't wet nor is the evening blonde

    Love   Switch off the moon

Don't drink your words
nor spill into my cup the bitter rings under your eyes
The morning to see you is sporting a tan

Switch on the sun   Love
and slay the evening dance

Otoño

A J. Chabás y Martí

Mujer densa de horas
y amarilla de frutos
como el sol del ayer

El reloj de los vientos te vio florecer
cuando en su jaula antigua
se arrancaba las plumas el terco atardecer

El reloj de los vientos
despertador de pájaros pascuales
que ha dado la vuelta al mundo
y hace juegos de agua en los advientos

De tus ojos la arena fluye en un río estéril
Y tantas mariposas distraídas
han fallecido en tu mirada
que las estrellas ya no alumbran nada

Mujer cultivadora
de semillas y auroras

Mujer en donde nacen las abejas
que fabrican las horas

Mujer puntual como la luna llena

Abre tu cabellera   origen de los vientos
que vacía y sin muebles
mi colmena te espera

Autumn

for J. Chabas y Martí

Woman thick with hours
and yellow with fruit
like yesterday's sun

The clock of the winds saw you flower
while in its ancient cage
the stubborn sunset yanked its feathers

The clock of the winds
alarm of Easter birds
that's rounded the world
spouting Advent's waters

From your eyes flows sand a barren river
And so many distracted butterflies
have perished in your gaze
stars no longer shed their light

Woman cultivating
seeds and dawns

Woman from whom bees buzz forth
who forge the hours

Woman punctual as the full moon

Part your tresses   origin of the winds
for empty and unfurnished
my hive awaits you

Noche de Reyes

A J. Díaz Fernández

El niño y el molino
han olvidado su único estribillo

Se ha callado la rueda en mi bemol
alrededor del pozo
por donde sube el agua y baja el sol

La mano en la mejilla
piensan las chimeneas que volarán un día

Hoy no vendrá la luna
ni pasará el borracho
entre el portal abierto y la canción de cuna

Aquí al pie del muro
fatigado del viaje
el viento se ha sentado

El policía lleno de fe
apunta las estrellas nuevas en el carnet

Y sin lograr atravesar el barrio
las fluviales carretas
cabecean en vano

Sólo cantan alegres las veletas

Las casas melancólicas
se peinan los tejados

Y una de ellas se muere
sin que nadie se entere

Twelfth Night

for J. Díaz Fernández

The boy and the mill
have forgotten their only refrain

The wheel's fallen silent at E flat
around the well
where water rises and the sun goes down

A hand on their cheeks
the chimneys think one day they'll fly

The moon won't arrive today
nor will the drunk stumble
past the open door and lullaby

Here at the foot of the wall
tired from the trip
the wind has taken a seat

The devout policeman jots
new stars down in his pad

And failing to cross these streets
the river carts
toss their heads in vain

Only the weather cocks sing their song

The gloomy houses
comb their roofs

And one of them is dying
and no one is noticing

Esta noche no viene la luna
ni el farol al borracho le sirve de cuna

The moon's not coming tonight
nor does the streetlamp cradle the drunk

Bahía

A Luis Corona

Las semanas emergen
del fondo de los mares
y las algas decoran los bares

Para que tú te alejes y yo pueda cantar
esperaremos el regreso
del viento de artificio y de la pleamar

Por eso
y con un ruido que no es el de otras veces
en la bahía ha anclado
tu melena enmohecida
violín para los peces
y para los suicidas

Venid a ver las nubes familiares
en mi taller todas las tardes
Son los naipes del cielo que nadie ha marchitado

El humo de la fábrica
hizo su nido en mi tejado
para los fumadores
que en la cartera llevan
en muestrario completo de habituales colores

Y mientras yo modelo mi retrato columna
sobre los montes delicados
pisa desnuda la lluvia

En las manos me deja
su corona de espinas
y cantando se aleja
sobre los techos y los climas

Bay

for Luis Corona

The weeks rise to the surface
from ocean depths
and taverns are draped with seaweed

For you to drift away and me to sing
we'll await the return
of high tide and a crafty wind

That is why
with a different sound than before
your mouldy hair has anchored
a violin in the bay
for fish and suicides

Come and see familiar clouds
afternoons in my shop
They are the sky's parched cards

Factory smoke
has nested on my roof
for the smokers
who carry in their wallets
a wide array of the usual colors

And while I model my column portrait
the rain treads
nude on the delicate hills

It leaves in my hands
its crown of thorns
and floats away singing
in the weather over roofs

Tu cabellera gime sin poder levar anclas

Embarcarme contigo
timonel de las galernas
Que el enjambre goloso de tus lluvias
se me pose en el hombro y en la pierna

Unable to weigh anchor your hair moans

Bring me aboard with you
at the helm of northwest winds
For your eager swarms of rain
settle on my shoulders and legs

Recital

Por las noches el mar vuelve a mi alcoba
y en mis sábanas mueren las más jóvenes olas

No se puede dudar
del ángel volandero
ni del salto de agua   corazón de la pianola

La mariposa nace del espejo
y a la luz derivada del periódico
yo no me siento viejo

Debajo de mi lecho
              pasa el río
y en la almohada marina
cesa ya de cantar el caracol vacío

Recital

At night the sea returns to my room
and the freshest waves die on my sheets

No one can doubt
the angel poised for flight
nor the spout of water   heart of the pianola

A butterfly flits out of the mirror
and in the light beaming from the daily paper
I don't feel old

Under my bed
        flows the river
and on my pillowed sea
the hollowed shell has stopped singing

Aldea

Del campanario va a volar el día
pero las nubes mías no han vuelto todavía

Ni han regresado los corderos
de su viaje a la luna sin pacer los luceros

                Aplicando el oído sobre el césped
                en vez del tren o el grillo
                se oye una pieza de organillo

Y el pastor no sabe
que en su cabaña está la noche
y que el molino es el motor del baile

Las vacas del establo
quieren lamer el sol
                      plato del día
                      que sirven los pintores de fantasía

                Es la hora del cigarro y de la jaula

Sin mirar al reloj pernocta el gallo
y las estrellas tristes contemplan al caballo

Village

The day will take flight from the belfry
though my clouds have yet to return

Nor are the lambs back from their trip
to the moon without grazing among the stars

                    Pressing your ear to the grass
                    it's not a train or a cricket you hear
                    but a barrel organ's tune

And a shepherd's unaware
the night is in his shed
and the mill's the motor of the dance

Cows in the stable
want to lick the sun

                              dish of the day
                            that inspires painters

                    It's time for a cigar and a cage

Ignoring the clock a rooster stays out all night
and gloomy stars gaze down at a horse

Hotel

A Alfonso Reyes

La frente sin laurel y sin sombrero
y el corazón para el color de moda

A cada nuevo baile
el reloj pierde el paso
y se equivoca de hora

El viento nace de tu manto
y acaricia las frutas
desgajadas del tango

Vendimia de las nubes pisoteadas
y de las músicas amadas

Y el ritmo de los suspiros
hace girar las parejas
y acercarse a nosotros el vestíbulo

Cerrando bien los ojos
pienso en las travesías
y en los hoteles que anclan la quilla envejecida

Son las islas trasatlánticas
donde crecen los mástiles
y dan frutos de invierno
donde los tísicos respiran
el oxígeno tierno

Al izar la bandera
esparce por los aires
plumas de cazadores y aromas de maderas

Hotel

for Alfonso Reyes

His head without a wreath or hat
and his heart's the color in vogue

With every new dance
the clock loses a beat
showing the wrong hour

The wind that blows from your cloak
caressing
the tango's plucked fruit

Harvest of crushed clouds
and beloved modes of music

And the rhythm of sighs
makes the couples twirl
luring the lobby closer

Tightly shutting my eyes
I picture voyages
hotels anchoring the old keel

They're islands like ocean liners
growing masts
abundant with winter fruit
where consumptives breathe
the tender oxygen

Upon hoisting the flag aromas
of wood are dispersed in the air
with the feathers of hunted birds

El otoño marchita corbatas y sombreros
y de la alfombra brota la primavera

Ruleta del azar y de las temporadas
Los jockeys de la moda sortean sus colores
Y aquel que pierde la jugada
tiene derecho a un vals para mudar de amores

Yo amo el buen tiempo y el hotel
y yo he visto mujeres de rizos calcinados
Las olas las rociaban de espumas de cocktail

Autumn shrivels ties and hats
and from the carpet blooms spring

Roulette of chance and the seasons
Fashion's jockeys raffle their colors
And whoever loses the bet
gets to waltz with a new lover

I love hotels and good weather
and I've seen women with roasted curls
The waves spraying them with cocktail foam

Canción de cuna

A Céline Arnauld

El viento de ida y vuelta
y el abanico en calma

El tren ha muerto en la estación de enfrente
y mi pañuelo cuelga de la rama más alta

Dejad que pasen los arroyos
Dejad que vuelen mis lágrimas
No permitáis en cambio que se acerquen
las ventanas lejanas

La noria seguirá
lavando los pañales
y la playa acunando
los náufragos triviales

Lullaby

for Céline Arnauld

The roundtrip wind
and the fan at rest

The train's expired at the station across the street
and my handkerchief hangs from the highest branch

Let the streams rush by
Let my tears fly away
But don't let the distant windows
come near

The waterwheel'll keep
washing the diapers
and the beach cradling
the trivial castaways

Vendimia

Leñador del ocaso
que perfumas los astros a tu paso

Guarda bien el compás   buen leñador
y ten piedad del sol caído
único salvavidas del rubio nadador

Guarda bien el compás
pero no cantes jamás

Canción bajo los árboles sin sangre
y frente al mar de luto
En el parque hay un árbol desleal
y mi poema en flor ya se ha hecho fruto

                         Leñador musical
Tu canción la ha aprendido mi loro pasional
y a su medida justa desfilan los minutos

Quién no sabe el secreto del color
Rasgar la túnica del viento
y arrancar del humo póstumo
la fruta del amor

Pero tú leñador de las estrellas
no derribes sus hojas sobre el mar
que cuando el sol rescate la antigua primavera
se han de secar tu brazo y tu cantar

Grape Harvest

Woodcutter at dusk
who perfumes the stars as you pass

Keep up the rhythm   good woodcutter
and pity the sunken sun
the blond swimmer's one lifesaver

Keep up the rhythm
but never ever sing

Song beneath a bloodless grove
before a grieving sea
In the park there's a disloyal tree
and my flowering poem's a fruit

                              Musical woodcutter
My passionate parrot's learned your song
and the minutes march to the beat of its rhythm

Who doesn't know color's secret
To shred the tunic of the wind
and pluck love's fruit
from posthumous smoke

But you woodcutter of the stars
don't scatter their leaves over the sea
for when the sun rescues ancient spring
your arm and your song will run dry

Adiós

Olvidados de la lluvia
se marchitarán mis dedos
No han de producir más flores
mis arrugados cabellos
ni la luna bajará
a coronarme el sombrero

Desde mañana
el sol ya no visita sus enfermos

Mujer
lavandera fragante
del vinoso atardecer
que grabaste en la luna tantas veces
los emblemas nupciales
y en un pico del mar mis iniciales

                Mujer

Cuando te alejes lenta sobre tu propia vida
veremos caer el sol
y las frutas podridas

Mientras tú bebas tus risas
balará mi acordeón
buscando entre los arbustos
ritmos de tu corazón

Los grillos contarán tus pasos diminutos

Ni la luna se hará llena
aunque me digas
                te quiero
ni ha de bajar ya la nieve
a bendecirme el sombrero

Goodbye

Forgotten by the rain
my fingers'll wither one day
My rumpled hair
won't sprout flowers anymore
nor will the moon descend
placing its crown on my hat

And from tomorrow on
the sun won't sit with the sick

Woman
fragrant laundress
in the wine-drenched dusk
who etched and etched on the moon
nuptial emblems
stitched my initials on a flap of the sea

                              Woman

When you drift slowly from your very life
we'll see the sun come down
and the rotting fruit drop

And as you sip your laughter
my accordion will baa
searching in the shrubs
the rhythms of your heart

Crickets will count your tiny steps

Nor will the moon grow full
even if you say
                      I love you
nor will the snow flutter down
blessing my hat

Novela

A Paul Dermée

La verja del jardín se ha cruzado de brazos

                El viento ladra entre los troncos

El auto que pasaba se llevó los sollozos
y apaciguó el estanque

Diríase que el sol
se ha burlado del parque

He aquí los tres policías
a investigar el rapto
buscando huellas de la huida
por las teclas del piano

A cada nuevo indicio
un pájaro falso traspone el edificio
y sometida al interrogatorio
una estrella muda marcha al suplicio

Prosigamos adelante

La infatigable carretera
va y viene sin cesar por la ladera
Son las cinco de la tarde
Junto al arroyo el agua
y a muy pocos kilómetros la primavera

La luna corre para llegar antes

Dónde están los amantes

Novel

for Paul Dermée

The garden gate has crossed its arms

                The wind barks in a grove of trunks

A passing car whisks away the sobs
calming down the lake

You could say the sun
has made fun of the park

And here are three detectives
looking into the abduction
dusting the piano keys
for getaway prints

With every uncovered clue
a fake bird disappears behind a building
and under intense questioning
a mute star stares down death

And on we go

The road never tires of departing
and returning alongside hills
It's five in the afternoon
Water sprawls next to a stream
and a few miles away   spring

The moon rushes to get there first

Where are the lovers

Apenas las esquinas ciudadanas
se despidieron
            hasta mañana
cuando se vio saltar de un coche
del brazo del traidor
la inesperada noche

El reloj de la torre dilató su pupila

Y los gallos despistados
cuentan una hora más de las precisas

En todos los rincones hay un bulto
y una luz cuelga del balcón
A cada paso del transeúnte
la luz cede y el cielo se resiente

Henos por fin ante el ladrón

El reloj ingenuo canta el crimen

Y entre el llorar de las cortinas
la luna estalla de pasión

La ciudad duerme en el sitio de costumbre

Y en el lugar del suceso
el farol asustado contempla al árbol preso

City corners hardly
said goodbye
              see you tomorrow
when you saw the sudden
night leap from an elbow
jutting treacherous from a passing car

The clock on the tower enlarged its pupil

And confused cocks
lose track of the added hour

There's a lump in every corner
and from the balcony hangs a lamp
With every step a passer-by takes
the light yields and the sky darkens

At last we've cornered the crook

A naïve clock confesses murder

And in the folds of the sobbing curtains
the moon bursts with passion

The city sleeps in the usual places

And at the scene of the crime
a spooked streetlight gazes at a caged tree

Nieve

La noche marchó en tren
y el ala de mi verso se abre y se cierra bien

Hoy los corderos amontonan la risa

Es el día sin mar

Nunca estuvo tan cerca
la mujer hermosa
y el árbol escolar

La nieve sube y baja
y las orugas hilan la mortaja

Snow

Night departed on a train
and the wing of my poem opens and closes well

Lambs pile up laughter today

It's a day without the sea

Never was the beautiful
woman so near
and a school tree

The snow rises and falls
and caterpillars spin a shroud

Panorama

El cielo está hecho con lápices de colores
Mi americana intacta no ha visto los amores
Y nacido en las manos del jardinero
el arco iris riega los arbustos exteriores

Un pájaro perdido anida en mi sombrero

Las parejas de amantes marchitan el parquet

Y se oyen débilmente las órdenes de Dios
que juega consigo mismo al ajedrez

Los niños cantan por abril
La nube verde y rosa ha llegado a la meta
Yo he visto nacer flores
entre las hojas del atril
y al cazador furtivo matar una cometa

En su escenario nuevo ensaya el verano
y en un rincón del paisaje
la lluvia toca el piano

Panorama

The sky's done up with crayons
My spotless jacket hasn't gazed upon love
and arcing from the gardener's hands
rainbows water the outdoor shrubs

A lost bird nests in my hat

The paired-off lovers wear down the parquet

And you barely hear God's instructions
playing chess against himself

Children sing for April
Green and rosy clouds reach the finish
I've seen flowers emerge
from between the pages on a music stand
and a hidden hunter slay a kite

Summer rehearses on its new stage
and in a corner of the countryside
the rain is playing the piano

Nubes

A Eugenio d'Ors

Yo   pastor de bulevares
desataba los bancos
y sentado en la orilla corriente del paseo
dejaba divagar mis corderos escolares

Todo había cesado
Mi cuaderno
             única fronda del invierno
y el kiosko bien anclado entre la espuma

Yo pensaba en los lechos sin rumbo siempre frescos
para fumar mis versos y contar las estrellas

Yo pensaba en mis nubes
                olas tibias del cielo
que buscan domicilio sin abatir el vuelo

Yo pensaba en los pliegues de las mañanas bellas
planchadas al revés que mi pañuelo

Pero para volar
es menester que el sol pendule
y que gire en la mano nuestra esfera armilar

Todo es distinto ya

Mi corazón bailando equivoca a la estrella
y es tal la fiebre y la electricidad
que alumbra incandescente la botella

Ni la torre silvestre
distribuye los vientos girando lentamente
ni mis manos ordeñan las horas recipientes

Clouds

for Eugenio d'Ors

I   shepherd of boulevards
would unleash the benches
and sitting on the lip of the promenade
release the lambs to roam

Everything had ground to a stop
My notebook
                 the only winter frond
and the newsstand anchored firmly in the foam

I'd think of the aimless beds forever fresh
where I smoked my poems and counted the stars

I'd think of my clouds
                     the sky's warm waves
looking for a home without ceasing to fly

I'd think of the lovely morning's pleats
like ironing my handkerchief unfolding it

But in order to soar
the sun needs to swing
and our heavenly globe revolve in our hands

Things are different now

My dancing heart deceives the star
and the fever the electricity is such
the bottle incandescently shines

Not even the wild tower turning slowly
distributes the winds
nor do my fingers milk the bowl-like hours

Hay que esperar el desfile
de las borrascas y las profecías
Hay que esperar que nazca de la luna
el pájaro mesías

Todo tiene que llegar

El oleaje del cine es igual que el del mar
Los días lejanos cruzan por la pantalla
Banderas nunca vistas perfuman el espacio
y el teléfono trae ecos de batalla

Las olas dan la vuelta al mundo
Ya no hay exploradores del polo y del estrecho
y de una enfermedad desconocida
se mueren los turistas
la guía sobre el pecho

Las olas dan la vuelta al mundo

Yo me iría con ellas

Ellas todo lo han visto
No retornan jamás ni vuelven la cabeza
almohadas desahuciadas y sandalias de Cristo

Dejadme recostado eternamente

Yo fumaré mis versos y llevaré mis nubes
por todos los caminos de la tierra y del cielo

Y cuando vuelva el sol en su caballo blanco
mi lecho equilibrado alzará el vuelo

We have to wait for the marching
 storms and prophecies
We have to wait for the moon to birth
the messiah bird

Everything has to arrive

The cinema's surf is the same as the sea's
Distant days flash across the screen
Flags never seen before perfume space
and echoes of war crackle on the phone

The waves swell around the world
No explorers left for poles and straits
and tourists are dying
of an unknown disease
guidebooks spread across their chests

The waves swell around the world

I'd love to ride along

They've seen it all
They never look back or return
evicted pillows sandals of Christ

Let me lie here till the end of time

I'll smoke my poems and lead my clouds
down every road on earth and in the sky

and when the sun returns on its white horse
my bed poised will lift off and fly

Cuadro

A Maurice Raynal

El mantel   jirón del cielo
es mi estandarte
y el licor del poniente
da su reflejo al arte

Yo prefiero el mar cerrado
y al sol le pongo sordina
Mi poesía y las manzanas
hacen la atmósfera más fina

Enmedio la guitarra

           Amémosla

Ella recoge el aire circundante
Es el desnudo nuevo
venus del siglo o madona sin infante

Bajo sus cuerdas los ríos pasan
y los pájaros beben el agua sin mancharla

Después de ver el cuadro
la luna es más precisa
y la vida más bella

El espejo doméstico ensaya una sonrisa
y en un trasporte de pasión
canta el agua enjaulada en la botella

Painting

for Maurice Raynal

The tablecloth   strip of the sky
is my flag
and the sunset's liquor
casts its reflection on art

I prefer an enclosed sea
on the sun I hang a shade
My poetry and apples
render the weather pure

In the middle the guitar

            Let us love her

She gathers the surrounding air
Is the modern nude
the century's venus or madonna without a child

Beneath her strings flow rivers
and birds drink without smudging the water

After viewing the painting
the moon is more precise
and life a little lovelier

Household mirrors rehearse a smile
and delirious with passion
water trapped in a bottle sings

Camino

A Jorge Guillén

Yo ya sé que es estéril
la rueda indagatoria
pero esta puerta de aspas será siempre mi noria

Las manos vacías suben
Las estrellas se van
Mis monedas son flores
y un día se mustiarán

Desde aquel día ya no habrá pastores

La calle cambia de postura
como mi barca semanal
La misma luna vive
de un ritmo vegetal

Dejemos el compás para el joven poeta
y a los astrónomos la ruleta
Las mariposas de hoy aman la oficina
Y esto no se interpreta
                    Nuevo día

Sin embargo yo soy el que ayer se moría
cuando cada farol era una herida mía

En la estación del alba
han fijado el cartel
El sol consulta diariamente su ruta
y se provee de miel

A la orilla gastada del camino
mi sombra y yo nos despedimos

Road

for Jorge Guillén

I know it's useless
the inquisitive reel
but this revolving door's my ferris wheel

Empty hands rise
Stars scatter
My coins are flowers
which one day'll wither

The day shepherds vanish

The street shifts
like my weekly boat
The moon itself lives
on vegetal rhythm

Let's give a compass to the young poet
and to astronomers a roulette
Today butterflies adore the office
and you can't interpret this
                      New day

Yet yesterday I stopped breathing
every streetlight a wound of mine

At dawn's station
they've hung the sign
The sun checks its daily route
providing honey of its own

On the road's worn shoulder
my shadow and I say goodbye

Y el tren que pasaba
ha dejado mis manos colmadas de racimos

And the passing train has left
my fists brimming with stems

Alegoría

Vedme aquí caminando sobre mi propio verso
como el barco de la tarde
que deja sobre el mar un reguero de sangre

No os acerquéis vosotros a escucharme

                      ganadores del pan
                      y del licor de amor

Ya murió el último intérprete
Llevaba en la mano la flor natural

          Belleza sin jornal
          Belleza clásica
          de mi violín estival

Los pájaros aprenden mis endecasílabos
la lluvia afina su guitarra enmohecida

Pasan bailando los días
Cada uno inventa una nueva figura
Y no creáis que esto es un juego

Es el verso sin humo
o el mar que se inaugura

Mi llave abre los trajes
y les extrae la carne interior

Corazón del vestido
Guardarropa y poesía sin dolor

Allegory

Here I am trampling my lines
like the boat of the afternoon
leaving in its wake a trail of blood

Stay away don't listen to me

                        winners of bread
                        and love's liquor

The last performer's just collapsed
Holding in his hand the natural flower

                  Beauty without a wage
                  My summer violin's
                  classical beauty

Birds learn the measure of my art
and the rain tunes its rusty guitar

Days go by dancing
Each one fashions a new shape
And don't you believe this is a game

It's smoke free verse
or the sea renewing itself

My key unlocks the suits
extracts their inner flesh

Heart of the dress
Cloakroom and poetry and no pain

Nocturno

A Manuel Machado

Están todas

También las que se encienden en las noches de moda

Nace del cielo tanto humo
que ha oxidado mis ojos

Son sensibles al tacto las estrellas
No sé escribir a máquina sin ellas

Ellas lo saben todo
Graduar el mar febril
y refrescar mi sangre con su nieve infantil

La noche ha abierto el piano
y yo las digo adiós con la mano

Nocturne

for Manuel Machado

They're all here

Even the ones that burn on fashionable nights

So much smoke descends from the sky
rust coats my eyes

Sensitive to the touch are the stars
I can't type without them

They know it all
How to raise the feverish sea
and cool my blood with its infant snow

Night has opened the piano
and I wave to them goodbye

Pasión penúltima

En su trineo bien atado
las golondrinas traen el viento
que encontraron en el pozo
                    durmiendo

Probablemente hoy cantarán los amantes
y harán vivo el espacio las estrellas errantes

Hoy se siente romántico
el reloj en mi pecho
Y mientras pasa el marino
fumando su destino
el viento hace nacer las alas de mi lecho

Es la hora decisiva
La única hora todavía viva

Árboles del camino
Mañana ensayaréis vuestro saludo en vano
Sin embargo
           algo queda

La estela de mi verso conduce al aeroplano
y los corderos llenan de humo la alameda

Penultimate Passion

Fastened tightly in their sled
the swallows bring the wind
they found in the well
                        sleeping

Lovers will probably sing today
wandering stars enliven space

Today the clock in my chest
feels romantic
And as a sailor strolls by
smoking his fate
the wind unfolds the wings of my bed

It is the crucial hour
the only hour still alive

Trees lining the road
Tomorrow you'll practice your greeting in vain
And yet
        something stays

The wake of my poem propels the plane
and the lambs fill the poplar grove with smoke

Eco

A Rodolfo Halffter

Repertorio del mar
Todos los días muda de programa y de traje

Cuánta música apócrifa
                        Cuánto color teñido
Y cómo copia el cielo
                su tela y su oleaje

Un velero naufraga
y canta y canta y canta mi pañuelo

Se va alejando el mar
A veces se inclina un poco a la derecha
Pero siempre son nuevos sus versos de romance
mar exangüe de tantos mástiles y flechas

Los peces laboriosos
trenzando y destrenzando estelas

Está ya viejo el mar
Ya no puede cantar

y los navíos que cruzan
se deshojan de malestar

El color es ya aroma
y la música brisa

El último naufragio hoy a las seis

Mi flauta y la luna
hacen la espuma

Echo

for Rodolfo Halffter

Repertoire of the sea
Each day another suit and show

The music so apocryphal
                    The color so dyed
And how it mimics the sky's
                    fabric and its waves

A sailboat sinks
and my handkerchief sings and sings and sings

The sea is drifting away
veering at times a bit to the right
Though the lyrics of its ballad are always new
exhausted sea of countless arrows and masts

The industrious fish
braiding and unbraiding wakes

The sea is old now
Can no longer sing

and the ships that cross
fall apart with malaise

Color is fragrance now
and music the breeze

The last shipwreck today at six

My flute and the moon
produce the foam

Lluvia

A G. Jean-Aubry

Puente arriba puente abajo
la lluvia está paseando
Del río nacen mis alas
y la luz es de los pájaros

Nosotros estamos tristes
Vosotros lo estáis también
Cuándo vendrá la primavera
a patinar sobre el andén

El invierno pasa y pasa
río abajo río arriba
Le ha visto la molinera
cruzar con la cabeza pensativa

El árbol cierra su paraguas
y de mi mano nace el frío
Pájaros viejos y estrellas
se equivocan de nido

Cruza la lluvia a la otra orilla
No he de maltratarla yo
Ella acelera el molino
y regula el reloj

El sol saldrá al revés mañana
y la lluvia vacía
volará a refugiarse en la campana

Rain

for G. Jean-Aubry

Bridge upstream bridge downstream
the rain's out for a stroll
The river unfolds my wings
and birds flash their lights

All of us are gloomy and sad
All of you are too
O when will spring arrive
to skate along this walkway

Winter passes and passes
river downstream river upstream
The miller's wife has seen it
pensively wade across

Trees shut their umbrellas
My hands spread the cold
Old birds and stars
mistake each others' nests

The rain reaches the opposite shore
I will not dismiss it
It quickens the mill
and regulates the clock

Tomorrow the sun will un-rise
and hollow drops of rain
swoop into the bell for refuge

Ventana

A José Bergamín

El violín descorre la cortina

Pende de un clavo la ventana

Aún está clausurado el paisaje

El sol   balón de oxígeno
mantiene puro el cuadro
y la lluvia hace el barnizaje

Esta casa está viva
Dos veces por minuto
la ventana respira

Y de mis manos surge
esta humareda votiva

En la pared el cuadro muere todos los años

Yo soy el pianista otoñal
Yo abro y cierro la noche como un libro
e interpreto la música
de mi cielo manual

                Podéis elegir
            La hora y la puerta

Pero después de amar hay que morir

El viento deja de nuevo en blanco mi cuaderno

Otra vez a empezar

No busquéis en el techo al planeta paterno

Window

for José Bergamín

The curtain opens to a violin

The window hangs from a nail

The countryside is still concealed

The sun   cylinder of oxygen
keeps the painting pristine
and the glazing's done by the rain

This house is alive
Twice in one minute
the window breathes

And from my hands rise
plumes of votive smoke

The painting on the wall dies every year

I am autumn's pianist
I open and close the night like a book
and play the music
in my handmade sky

                You can choose
                The time and the door

But once you've loved you have to die

Once more the wind has left my pages white

So again I begin

Don't scan the ceiling for fatherly planets

Espectáculo

A Francisco Vighi

A la derecha un resplandor

Es el rubor del cielo
o el calcetín inmaculado
arco iris del suelo

Todo está intacto

El pichón aprende el canto
y las reglas del vuelo
Hoy se renueva el río y el amor sin pacto

La música dirige el concilio de dioses
y la luna hace el entreacto

                Otra vez el mar

Se ha declarado en huelga
y no quiere acompañar

El piloto descuida la estrella y el violín
y mi mano abanica los veleros cansados

Es como un solo de jardín
entre el murmullo de los prados

                Buenos días

Es la primera vez que sale el sol sin hacer ruido

Y yo consulto en la guía
dónde se hace el trasbordo sin cambiar de vestido

Performance

for Francisco Vighi

Off to the right a radiant glow

It's the sky blushing
or the immaculate sock
the ground's rainbow

Everything is intact

A pigeon learns the song
and the rules of flight
Today the river and love are renewed without a pact

Music directs the council of gods
and the moon plays an interlude

                Once more the sea

It's gone on strike
refusing to play along

A pilot neglects the star and violin
my hand fans the tired skiffs

It's like a garden solo
in a rustling meadow

                Good morning

The first time without making a sound the sun has risen

And I consult the guide
to transfer without changing clothes

Pasan las horas llevando mi equipaje
No sé si llegaré a tiempo al desenlace

Las estrellas se relevan por turno

                      Última hora

            Un instante se ha visto

                Era el astro anular
                o la aureola de Cristo

El bosque y la orquesta lloran

En mi reloj son las cuatro

Cae sobre el mar la lluvia
como un telón de teatro

The hours go by carrying my luggage
Will I reach the ending on time

Stars shine in shifts

        At last

     A moment's been seen.

        It was an eclipsed star
        or the halo of Christ

The forest and orchestra weep

My watch says it's four

Rain falls over the sea
like a stage curtain

Mostly Madrid

a braided collage
for Emilio Sanz de Soto (1924–2007)

The glossy poster announced, "*an evening with John Ashbery.*" The bookshop's bulletin board grabbed my attention indeed. I remember thinking as I stepped outside: I am *there*. In the end, a friend's invitation to journey north to San Sebastian proved more enticing than a poetry reading at the U.S. embassy. I can count on one hand the literary events I attended during the years I lived in Madrid. Which is not to say poetry never crossed my mind. Over the span of my decade in Spain, I was reading it, translating it, trying my own hand at it.

*

I step off the curb and into the street to scan the oncoming traffic. I spot a green light in the distance and wave my arm above my head. The approaching vehicle slows to a stop. I return to the curb to fetch Emilio, walk him to the waiting cab—white sedan, diagonal red stripe across its door. I help Emilio in, get in myself.

—Por favor, la Residencia de Estudiantes.

*

In 1922 three young men coincided at la Residencia de Estudiantes. One, fascinated with insects and drums, was from the region of Aragón. Another, from a whitewashed village north of Barcelona, liked to sketch. A third played the piano and wrote poems about his native Andalusia. They were away at college in Madrid, met and became friends. Nothing remarkable there, unless we consider who they became: Oscar-winning filmmaker, Luis Buñuel; flamboyant visual artist, Salvador Dalí; renowned poet and playwright, Federico García Lorca.

*

La Residencia de Estudiantes is a venerated space in Spanish culture. Modelled after Cambridge and Oxford, it was founded as a place to nurture a cultural elite. In 1924, the year its lecture society formed, la Residencia was a magnet for writers, scholars, and artists. The roster was impressive: Albert Einstein, Madame Curie, H. G. Wells, Paul Valéry, Maurice Ravel, Filippo Tommaso Marinetti to name a few. It ceased functioning during the Franco dictatorship. It began its long recuperation in 1983.

For a time, la Residencia housed the Fundación Federico García Lorca before it relocated south to Granada, the poet's hometown. La Residencia is home to multiple archives and still welcomes scholars and artists from various disciplines. It also continues to present cultural events. In fact, la Residencia de Estudiantes hosted several sessions of the Unamuno Authors Festival in 2019, a gesture spearheaded by the American poet Spencer Reece, a resident of Madrid at the time. The gathering featured dozens of anglophone poets and scholars.

Although Emilio has not provided a street address, our driver knows our destination very well. Our taxi is heading north, up one of Madrid's main arteries, Paseo de la Castellana. It is June 9, 1989. Emilio and I are on our way to see Octavio Paz.

*

I've often spoken about John K. Walsh—Jack, my mentor at UC Berkeley. During those years, the mid nineteen eighties, he was also mentoring a PhD candidate named Carolyn Tipton. Aware of my interest in Lorca and other poets of his generation, Jack would sometimes mention Tipton's project to me. She was rendering into English the Spanish poet Rafael Alberti. He'd gone into exile at the outbreak of the Spanish Civil War. After a brief stint in Paris, Alberti spent the bulk of his years in Argentina until 1963. He later resided in Italy before returning to Spain in 1977, two years after the dictator's death.

A la pintura / To Painting, published in 1998, was Carolyn Tipton's brilliant rendering of Rafael Alberti's book of poems devoted to the visual arts. Unbeknownst to Tipton, early on Jack had been letting me read her translations. He'd loaned me the copy of her dissertation that she'd given to him—signed with an affectionate dedication.

On December 4, 1987, Alberti read from these poems at the Instituto Internacional in Madrid. I was spending the academic year in Barcelona but had the habit of stealing back to the capital for days at a time when my schedule allowed it. This was one of those times.

Rafael Alberti gripping two canes, one in each hand, slowly making his entrance up the center aisle, his abundant white hair reaching his shoulders… is what looms in memory. He was helped into a chair, Carolyn Tipton beside him, both of them sitting at a table, facing the audience. Every seat in the house was filled. Alberti's voice, rich and grave and well-amplified, mesmerized us all—in poem after poem. Tipton's own voice joined his, weaving her translations into their braided presentation. I remember being enthralled by the pieces addressed to the colors of the spectrum. If the poetry bug had bitten me back in Berkeley, that evening in Madrid a blistering fever took hold. I was 21.

*

Emilio and I arrive early. La Residencia's brick pavilions are nestled at the end of a long driveway, hidden almost, in an enclave of trees. You almost forget you're in the heart of modern Madrid. By the time the event is set to commence it's standing-room only. Octavio Paz is seated at a table with three microphones. I am sitting between Emilio and Javier Aguirre—a friend we spotted as we made our way to our seats near the front, the rows of chairs arrayed across a level wooden floor.

On occasion, after a screening at the Filmoteca—typically a black and white classic—Emilio and I would run into Javier Aguirre. We'd invariably slip into a nearby café for a visit. Aguirre was a filmmaker. He wrote and directed slapstick movies as a means of funding his less commercial projects. His film on Che Guevara was called *Che, Che, Che*. Another was inspired by a suite of poems by Fernando Pessoa. One, a dramatic monologue by his wife, the actress Esperanza Roy, was filmed on a beach with her sitting in a chair.

Aguirre is partial to Octavio Paz's surrealism. Chatting with him after the reading, we both agree on the piece we most enjoyed: a deliciously delivered 'Fábula de Joán Miró,' a sublime homage to the Catalan artist.

**

I've come to believe we experience certain works of art when we most need them. It's been that way for me—poets whose words I return to, again and again.

**

The first time I saw Seamus Heaney people were sitting in the aisles. This was after my year abroad in Barcelona. I had to return to Berkeley to finish up with some breadth requirements.

I was seated way in the back, the sound-system meagre—I could barely hear the poet. Dwinelle Hall was so packed I began to perspire.

When I was back in Spain the following year, I sat down with his debut collection, *Death of a Naturalist*. I'd picked up the Faber edition at an English-language bookshop and walked to a nearby café. As I was reading the poems, it became clear: I was meant to re-encounter Seamus Heaney. In the months that followed I read through *Door into the Dark, Wintering, North, Field Work, Station Island*, and *The Haw Lantern*. This latest title from 1987—the year I first stepped onto the tarmac at Barajas airport. It was August, the month after the Spanish poet, Gerardo Diego, died in his home in Madrid—a flat I would set foot in a decade later to meet Elena Diego, his daughter.

But it was *Seeing Things*, Heaney's next book from 1991, that occasioned an especially meaningful moment. After buying it, I learned that the Irish poet would be making a presentation in Madrid. I decided to give a Seamus Heaney poetry reading another try.

There we were—the elegant marble columns of the Círculo de Bellas Artes surrounding us. It was the launch of his selected poems, translated into Spanish. There was something about the intimacy of the event: forty of us in attendance, no more—the master poet at the top of his form in poem after poem, first in his carefully paced English, y después en español: the voice of his translator.

Two years before that magical evening with Heaney, I'd begun an MA in Hispanic Civilization—a one-year program with New York University. In truth, it was an excuse to get back to Spain. And yet, "NYU in Spain" proved to be a solid fit: it offered literary translation as a way to complete the required thesis. NYU's classrooms and offices were at the Instituto Internacional—steps away from the Rubén Darío metro station.

*

After Octavio Paz performs his final poem, after most of the public has departed the premises, Emilio and I part, and step through, a plush curtain: a table of tapas and bottles of wine await two dozen guests for a private reception. We are standing in groups of three or four, chilled shrimp and glass of wine in hand. The poet is circulating from one cluster of guests to another.

Octavio Paz walks towards us. Emilio extends a hand in greeting. They had met on a previous occasion and the expression on Paz's face is one of recognition. Emilio proceeds to introduce me as "el traductor de los sonetos del amor oscuro de Lorca." He adds that Lorca's *Collected Poems*, published with FSG, is the first venture of its kind: a Spanish-language poet having all their poetry published in English. (Where Emilio got this tidbit of information I don't know. Later it occurs to me that he was making it up.)

To which Paz responds by saying that New Directions published *his Collected Poems* before Lorca's. Emilio counters: But Señor Paz, one would assume that you have not finished writing all of your poetry! The poet shifts his gaze and floats a question in my direction. I notice his eyes are hazel. My parents, I answer, migrated to San Francisco in the late fifties from Managua.

*

When it came time to determine who I would translate for my thesis, my aim was to select a poet from la generación del '27—in other words, a contemporary of Lorca's. Emilio, early on, had introduced me to José Teruel Benevente, a Spanish poet-critic, maybe ten years my senior, who, like Emilio, taught in the NYU program. We would sometimes coincide with Pepe at a popular gathering space—entering the Instituto, facing the central staircase, one could pivot right and walk down a different, narrower set of stairs into what was, in effect, a basement café, a place where students and professors alike could grab coffee and a snack, which served a daily special. One afternoon, the three of us were seated around one of its small square tables. Emilio and Pepe were pondering out loud who I might translate. My desire, I said, is that it be a poet whose work wasn't available in English. Something clicked because Pepe paused, and then pronounced:

> —Debes de traducir a Gerardo Diego, una de sus obras creacionistas… ya lo tengo: *Manual de espumas*.

*

I brought *Seeing Things* to the Círculo de Bellas Artes. I was still in sporadic touch with Robert Pinsky, with whom I'd taken a workshop in Berkeley. By then he was at BU. Once, in a note to me, he mentioned "Seamus" as one of the reasons he enjoyed being in Boston. Heaney was teaching at Harvard at the time. As I waited in line to have my book signed, I debated whether or not I should mention I was Pinsky's former student.

—What's your name, Seamus Heaney asked, as I handed him the book.

I answered, and then mentioned how much I enjoyed his poems in both languages. After he inscribed his book, he held it against his chest, his body language suggesting he wasn't going to return it anytime soon.

—What brings you to Madrid, he asked.

—Uh, I completed a Masters here a couple of years ago, and I'm teaching English as a Foreign Language now.

Pause.

—I mean your writing, your poems. What's your plan, he gently prodded.

His question conveyed: Okay, you've told me you studied with Robert Pinsky. Tell me more. There was no one standing behind me so I relaxed a bit.

*

And then the following exchange with Octavio Paz:

—Ah, Nicaragua, a country of poets! Tell me, Francisco: what Nicaraguan poet do you admire?

—I've read Ernesto Cardenal (A second after Cardenal's name leaves my lips I remember Paz is anti-Sandinista and his response doesn't surprise me).

—Hmm, yes, an interesting writer, though I find much of his work political propaganda.

—The work of his I admire most are his love poems, his epigrams (I say this knowing they are pre-revolution, though they happen to be the work I'm most drawn to).

—Yes, those are nice, though they seem derivative of Pound.

—Well, he translated a lot of Pound so it doesn't surprise me he'd be influenced by him, or Williams, who he also read at Columbia.

—Yes, William Carlos Williams is a wonderful poet, and do you know what American poet was at Columbia when Cardenal was there?

—Thomas Merton he studied with in Kentucky so I guess it couldn't have been him... I suppose... that would've been... Allen Ginsberg...

(I can hardly believe this conversation is taking place.)

—What other Nicaraguan poets have you read? (It doesn't escape my notice that he's asked in the plural)

—I've enjoyed some of José Coronel Urtecho's work, but probably the poet I most admire after Cardenal is Pablo Antonio Cuadra, though I also like Daisy Zamora.

—Ahhhh yes, he is truly an indigenous poet, muy indio....

at which point a woman in gown and pearls appears and places her hand on Paz's elbow to signal that the next cluster of admirers awaits his presence. Days later, Emilio would say to me that he'd never heard of the Nicaraguan poets I'd mentioned to Paz, and how delighted he was to listen in on my brief exchange with the Mexican poet.

*

Emilio Sanz de Soto: independent film scholar. He had received in the mail two invitations to the Octavio Paz event as an honorary "amigo de la Residencia." I was one of his students, enrolled in 'The films of Luis Buñuel and Carlos Saura.' During his first lecture, he had made a passing reference to Ezra Pound so I approached him after class. He promptly suggested I join him for a drink at Bar Miguel Ángel across the street. It was the beginning of a friendship that would flourish all the years I lived in Spain.

One night, a few years ago, overcome with nostalgia for this singular connection, I googled Emilio Sanz de Soto. A native of Malaga, and a long-time resident of Tangiers in the mid twentieth century, he was considered the go-to person for any writer or artist passing through the Moroccan city. Among his coterie: Truman Capote, Tennessee Williams, Gore Vidal, Paul and Jane Bowles. He eventually returned to Madrid to teach for "NYU in Spain." Emilio died in 2007 at the age of 83. His personal papers, his archive, reside at la Residencia de Estudiantes.

*

Taking José Teruel's advice, I walk to the Rubén Darío metro station and mount the descending escalator, hopping on the green line to travel beneath the streets of Madrid until I reach Gran Via. Casa del Libro is one block away, where I buy the Cátedra edition of *Manual de espumas*, a bright work of cubist art donning the black cover. The next day, paperback in hand, I enter the Instituto and make my way down those narrow stairs, grabbing a table in the corner. I crack open Gerardo Diego and start reading 'Primavera,' the first poem. Something compels me to start whispering it to myself until I reach the end. Wow. I mouth the second poem. Wow. I softly say the third, the fourth, the fifth… as the sound of spoons touching porcelain and the chattering around me begin to recede. I lose track of noise and time taking in every poem—thirty in all, the last one titled 'Espectáculo.' When I finish, I look up at the clock on the wall as I begin to hear again the din of the room. If someone had walked up to my table in that basement café to ask what the poems were *about*, I would have shrugged. Later, I think to myself: What had been so fun about reading and saying those poems aloud?

*

I told Seamus Heaney about not returning to California after obtaining the MA; about the light teaching load that allowed me to write; how I still harbored doubts about my decision to remain in Madrid; how I loved living in Spain, travelling to all of its regions; about the first time I heard him in that sweaty Berkeley lecture hall.

Heaney stood there, patiently absorbing my torrent of speech. I finally forced my lips to stop moving. I saw his fingers relax—I looked at the book, his book, that he was still holding to his chest. His gaze softened as he began handing it back to me. Leaning in, he spoke—just above a whisper.

*

When I let NYU know I would be translating Gerardo Diego, I was assigned, as my thesis advisor, Louis Bourne—an older PhD candidate in his early fifties who resided in Madrid. He was finishing a dissertation on Rubén Darío. But he was also an experienced translator. My introduction to his work in this vein, *The Crackling Sun*, was a selected poems by the Spanish Nobel laureate Vicente Aleixandre, a contemporary of Lorca's. The book included Bourne's critical study of Aleixandre's oeuvre. The volume clocked in at nearly two hundred pages. I loved it. Bourne's mode of thesis advising? Dinner for two and a bottle of wine. We'd meet in his favorite

Chinese restaurant every two months. In addition to going over, and offering feedback on, drafts of my Diego translations, our sessions were sprawling conversations on poetry, on *translating* Spanish poetry.

*

Seamus Heaney's words were just what I needed:

—Congratulations Francisco. Keep doing what you're doing. You'll be fine.
My life in Madrid would unfold for another seven years.

*

I push open the elevator's glass-paneled doors, stepping onto the landing. The solid wooden front door is a few feet away. I'm five minutes early. Alberto Vera, a long-time friend, has arranged a special meeting. He lives just north of central Madrid and as luck would have it, his neighbor is Elena Diego. Our meeting is taking place where her mother—Gerardo Diego's French widow—still resides, the block of flats a short walk from the Instituto Internacional. It is 1997—ten years after the poet's death, ten years after I first set foot in Spain.

I first met Alberto, a retired law professor, in the summer of 1987. We were both browsing book stalls in el Retiro—Madrid's iconic park. We reconnected, in earnest, when I returned to Madrid to do my MA in 1989. One Saturday, he invited me to join him at the Gijón, the well-known café. He introduced me to a few of his friends. They would convene there weekly at 4 PM. As we rose, two hours later to say our goodbyes, they extended a standing invitation to come again—to join their *tertulia*. This became my Saturday routine. Topics of conversation would range from books to movies to politics to art, often with a healthy dose of humor. Here is where, for example, I learned what was well-known in certain circles: the Mexican poet, Amado Nervo, "era una loca." 'Tertulia' would go on to appear in *Puerta del Sol*, my first book of poems.

One Saturday, I mentioned that I was translating Gerardo Diego. Alberto piped that Elena Diego, the poet's daughter, lived in his building. He made it plain: if I ever wanted to meet her, just say the word and he'd make it happen. It would be years before I'd take him up on his gracious offer.

My thesis was twenty poems from *Manual de espumas*—rendered into English, along with a lengthy commentary. At first, I was on the fence about translating the remaining ten pieces. But Seamus Heaney's encouragement was the spark that spurred me to pursue this companion project, alongside my own poems. So I set myself the task of doing a deep dive—not only with Gerardo Diego, but with avant-garde movements in the arts in general, especially during, and shortly after, World War I.

I consulted primary sources in the Instituto Internacional's library. I got to hold in my hands the pocket-sized, first edition of *Manual de espumas* from 1924. I also gained access to the Biblioteca Nacional to further my research. In 1996, to celebrate the centenary of Gerardo Diego's birth, the National Library organized an exhibition, 'Gerardo Diego and Spanish Poetry in the 20th Century.' Once, around this time, I asked to see the 1970 edition of his "selected poems." In the preface he wrote to the selection from *Manual de espumas*, Diego wrote (my translation):

> *Handbook of Foams*, where creationist poetics are concerned, is my classic book. Long conversations with Vicente Huidobro and Juan Gris, as well as Maria Blanchard, Léger, and other artists, critics, and poets who were in Paris that year made it possible for me to learn what I needed. As I listened to them, though, I kept thinking about my music and my musicians, and I would mentally translate plastic terms to a temporal and successive vocabulary which, by being so, became more ideal for composing poetry. The rapports, the gradual change of a natural object or theme until it transfigures into a unit, and its autonomous qualities, both plastic and chromatic—all of these revealed a range of perspectives, views which later found their poetic corollary on a Cantabrian beach.

Plucking this passage of prose spurred me further. These were the years I read with relish, Guillaume Apollinaire, Pierre Reverdy, Louis Aragon, and others. These were the years I discovered Juan Larrea. These were the years I devoured Vicente Huidobro and César Vallejo.

In fact, I grew increasingly drawn to, and fascinated by, poets from the Americas who spent extended periods of time in Europe. I sometimes wondered how I might fit into such a lineage—the son of Nicaraguan immigrants, born and raised in California, who migrated to Spain.

*

At 4 PM, I ring the bell. A young woman opens the door and asks me to follow her, leading me down a corridor into an elegantly furnished drawing room. Elena Diego, a woman in her fifties, soon appears and greets me. She takes a seat at a table, gesturing for me to join her. The young woman reappears, this time with a tray of coffee, water, and pastries, setting it down. I have brought with me two literary journals, shipped to me from the United States—*Nimrod*, and my extra copy of *Chelsea*, which I will leave with Ms. Diego. After initial pleasantries, and a chat about our mutual friend, Alberto Vera, I fish the journals out of my shoulder bag and set them on the table. One at a time, I show Elena Diego some English versions of her father's poems. As I am turning to the designated pages, I say, somewhat sheepishly, that I was deliberate about never seeking to publish the Spanish originals—only my translations. I had taken up Alberto's offer to connect us, I say, because my residence in Spain was coming to an end. I tell her that I will soon be departing for California. I share my goal of finding a publisher for a translation of *Manual de espumas* and that I would like her blessing. I reveal that I've been in correspondence with José Luis Bernal Salgado, who has written extensively about her father, that he has been very helpful. I report that I attended a summer symposium in Santander and had the pleasure of meeting a number of *hispanistas* who have published widely on her father's poetry. Elena Diego listens attentively. She thanks me for my efforts. And then, unprompted, says that I may continue to place my English translations in magazines, but that I should contact her if a publisher ever becomes interested in doing a dual-language book. Formal permission would need to be secured. My encounter with her lasts just shy of an hour.

*

The upper, left-hand corner of the busy festival poster included this snippet of text:

> 80 readings
> 5 venues
> 1 week

The Unamuno Authors Festival in Madrid unfolded from May 27 to June 1, 2019. Its various venues included Desperate Literature—a multilingual bookshop, the Instituto Internacional, and la Residencia de Estudiantes.

The 7 PM session at la Residencia on May 30 opened with Laura García Lorca, the poet's niece. She delivered a moving *testimonio* that included reading out loud a letter penned by her uncle, Federico—an epistle he wrote from la Residencia while in college. In the letter—addressed to his father—Federico García Lorca defends with passion his chosen path in the arts. The program that night also featured a young poet from Fresno, California, Steven Sanchez, who had just been awarded the Lorca Latinx Poetry Prize for an Emerging Poet. Sharing the stage that evening to also read their poetry were Afro-Latina poet, Aracelis Girmay, Spanish poet, Luis Muñoz, and myself.

At the reception afterwards, held in the courtyard, I expressed to Laura and Luis how meaningful it was to be at la Residencia. The last time I was here, I said, was in 1989—to see Octavio Paz. I was with a dear friend: Emilio Sanz de Soto. Laura and Luis looked at one another. She reached out and gently held my arm as she recalled her multiple encounters with Emilio over the years, how she had cherished and relished his storytelling. Luis, listening, promptly spoke up, as well.

In the years before Emilio Sanz de Soto's death, Luis Muñoz held a job at la Residencia. One of his most memorable experiences, he told us, was befriending, and working with, Emilio when it was decided that his personal papers would be archived at la Residencia. When Luis concluded his *testimonio* on the heels of Laura's, the three of us stood there—dwelling in this fortuitous coincidence, awash with affection for our absent and beloved friend.

Earlier that evening, I had stepped to the podium and opened with two pieces from *Puerta del Sol*—my book of poems set mostly in Madrid. But during my decade in Spain, translation also became an integral part of my artistic practice. And so I also read 'Emigrante,' followed by 'Emigrant,' my English rendering of Gerardo Diego—one of my favorites from *Handbook of Foams*.

July 2025
Carlsbad, CA

Publication credits

Gratitude to the editors of the publications where all of these translations previously appeared, sometimes in earlier versions:

ANMLY (online): 'Rain'

Ariel: 'Fountain' and 'Twelfth Night'

Beltway Poetry Quarterly (online): 'Echo,' 'Road,' and 'Rhyme'

Chelsea: 'Fountain' and 'Snow'

The Cortland Review (online): 'Novel'

Jacket (online): 'Hotel,' 'Emigrant,' 'Goodbye,' 'Clouds,' 'Autumn,' 'Twelfth Night,' 'Panorama,' 'Allegory,' 'Window,' and 'Recital'

Luna: 'Table,' 'Emigrant,' 'Village,' and 'Penultimate Passion'

Nimrod: 'Recital,' 'Nocturne,' and 'Autumn'

The Packinghouse Review: 'Spring,' 'Bay,' and 'Echo'

Poetry International Online: 'River Song,' 'Grape Harvest,' and 'Performance'

Skyblue: 'Penultimate Passion'

'Performance,' 'Paradise,' and 'Rain' appeared in the anthology *Written in Arlington* (Paycock Press, 2020), edited by Katherine Young

'Painting,' 'Spring,' 'Lookout,' 'Road,' 'Lullaby,' 'Rhyme,' 'Bay,' and 'Echo' were published in *Achiote Seeds* in its Achiote Press Chapbook Division, alongside Javier Huerta, Veronica Montes and Mónica de la Torre, edited by Craig Santos Perez and Jennifer Remer

Some pieces from *Handbook of Foams* appeared in volume 16/17 of *The Chaminade Literary Review*.

An earlier version of the introduction, 'Contexualizing *Handbook of Foams*,' appeared in *Jacket* no. 40, founded and edited by John Tranter.

An earlier version of the essay, 'Mostly Madrid' (as 'In Madrid') appeared in *Desperate Literature, The Unamuno Author Series Festival: A Bilingual Anthology*.

Gratitude

A portion of *Handbook of Foams* was my MA thesis for NYU. The late Emilio Sanz de Soto, film historian and writer, and Louis Bourne, American poet and translator, were crucial mentors.

Henry Reese, founder of City of Asylum in Pittsburgh, PA, provided a residency on Sampsonia Way where the introductory essay was extensively revised.

Caridad Moro-Gronlier, the poet, facilitated an 'Escribe Aquí / Write Here' residency at The Betsy Hotel in Miami, FL where some of these translations were revised.

Institutions in Spain that had a role in my gaining a better grasp of the milieu that nourished Gerardo Diego include: the Instituto Internacional, whose library in Madrid I consulted; the Biblioteca Nacional, which granted me access to its collections and hosted an exhibition in Madrid on Gerardo Diego; the Universidad Internacional Menéndez Pelayo in Santander, which held a summer symposium on Gerardo Diego, where I met and conversed with: José Luis Bernal Salgado, whose book, *Manual de espumas: La plenitud creacionista de Gerardo Diego* was essential; Francisco Díez de Revenga, whose article, '*Manual de espumas* y el creacionismo' was also key; and Italian *hispanista* Gabriele Morelli, whose edited volume, *Treinta años de vanguardia española* got me started.

The CantoMundo gathering in Tempe, AZ was where I revised and expanded 'Mostly Madrid,' the concluding essay. The Macondo Writers Workshop in San Antonio, TX was where I put the finishing touches on the manuscript before submitting it to Shearsman Books.

I would like to document—for my record—friends who were supportive of this project during the years I lived in Spain—namely, the members of my Saturday afternoon *tertulia* at the café Gijón in Madrid: the late Alberto Vera, the late Oscar Yañez, the late José Antonio Marañon.

Two individuals at the University of Notre Dame, whose sensibilities nourished me in relation to this project while I was an MFA candidate there include: John Matthias, whose poetry workshop was grounded in translation; Steve Fredman whose poetics seminar (team-taught with Gerald Bruns) was especially valuable.

The late poet, editor, and anthologist, John Tranter, was a champion of *Handbook of Foams*, and offered valuable feedback on some of these translations.

Tony Frazer's translations of Vicente Huidobro convinced me that Shearsman Books was the right place for Gerardo Diego. Thank you for saying yes.

Elena Diego, the poet's daughter, granted Shearsman Books permission, all these years later—after I sat in her home in Madrid one afternoon to show her first renderings of her father's poems. *Gracias*!

Francisco Aragón
San Antonio, TX
July 2025

Biographical sketches

GERARDO DIEGO (1896–1987) is arguably the least known Spanish poet of the renowned "generation of '27," which included Federico Garcia Lorca, Rafael Alberti, Pedro Salinas, Jorge Guillén and Luis Cernuda to name a few. With the exception of Lorca, who was executed at the outbreak of the Spanish Civil War, these others went into exile, which may explain, in part, why Diego is less known. And yet Diego was among the most active in his cohort, having the foresight to edit the ground-breaking and prophetic *Spanish Poetry Anthology 1915–1931*, in which he gathers this generation of poets for the first time, as well as some of their immediate mentors. He was also among the most fervent of this cohort to explore and embrace the avant-garde tendencies of his time, particularly *creacionismo*, which he alternates throughout his writing career with more traditional verse forms, making him unique. He also edited two journals: *Carmen: a little magazine of Spanish poetry*, and *Lola: Carmen's friend and supplement*. Over the course of his career, his many books won all the major poetry prizes in Spain and he shared the Cervantes Prize with Jorge Luis Borges in 1979. An accomplished pianist and music critic, his day job throughout his professional life was as a high-school French teacher. The last project to occupy Diego was the preparation of his two-volume *Poetry*. He completed the task, but his death on the afternoon of July 8, 1987, a month short of his 91st birthday, prevented him from holding the handsome hefty volumes, which finally appeared in 1989. In 1996, on the occasion of the centenary of his birth, various acts and exhibitions were organized, among them one at the National Library in Madrid titled *Gerardo Diego and Spanish Poetry in the 20th Century*.

FRANCISCO ARAGÓN is the son of Nicaraguan immigrants. A native of San Francisco, California, he is the author of three books of poetry: *Puerta del Sol* (2005), *Glow of Our Sweat* (2010) and *After Rubén* (2020), as well as editor of the anthology, *The Wind Shifts: New Latino Poetry* (2007). As a translator from the Spanish, he has had a hand in a number of books, including volumes by Francisco X. Alarcón (1954–2016), Federico García Lorca (1888–1936) as a co-translator, and now Gerardo Diego (1896–1987). In recent years, he has been elaborating English versions and trans-creations after Rubén Darío (1867–1916). He is on the faculty of the University of Notre Dame's Institute for Latino Studies, where he directs their literary initiative, *Letras Latinas*. He divides his time between South Bend, Indiana and Carlsbad, California. For more information, visit: http://franciscoaragon.net

www.ingramcontent.com/pod-product-compliance
Lightning Source LLC
Chambersburg PA
CBHW031407160426
43196CB00007B/926